Had I Become the Sun

poems by G. Lafayette

Copyright © 2025 G. Lafayette

All rights reserved.

ISBN: 979-8-218-69988-8

Dedication

Santico,
for what we were, for what we couldn't be,
and for everything that found its way into these pages.

*"Life is full of highs and lows;
the lows are what make the highs so beautiful."*

Table of Contents

Prelude	i
Echo	1
I	**2**
The End	3
Knowing	4
Bones	5
Grief	6
Like Her	7
The Gap	8
Red	9
One Second	10
Regrets	11
II	**13**
Voices	14
Betrayal	16
Holding On	18
Gone	19
Withdrawal	20

After	21
You (Part I)	22
Secrets	24
Exposed	25
The Message	26
Hesitation	27
Hope	28
III	**30**
To Liv	31
The Wish | Fate	32
You (Part II)	33
Too Much | Roses	34
One Day	36
How To Let Go	38
The Museum	40
Lilith	41
Epilogue	**42**
The Sun	43
Acknowledgements	**44**
About the Author	**47**

Prelude

*i never wanted to be known
as a calamity*

Echo

it takes everything in me
not to flinch
years pass
yet the echo lingers
a stain imprinted on my memories

they say i can revise the past
rewrite it for a happier end

how do i change the betrayal?
how do i accept your lies
became more important than truth?

if it begins
and ends with me
who's to say
i'm not at fault?

when they look back
at the ruins of your heart
will they name this disaster
after me?

I

*what happens when you're faced with
the reality of me
not the idea?*

The End

if i were strong enough
i would unearth the land
rebuild a home you
denied needs saving
but my flight is about to land
and you're in another tail spin

my love aches the way a cemetery
makes breathing look beautiful

everything my hands touch
haunts me in the end

Knowing

since i was a child
it was always following me
the raven
the sword
from a distance
they look no different

two worlds
and i wield both
this blood on my hands
belongs to them and
they're screaming my name

from the gallows to the stands
i am forced to play a role
poet
soldier
saint
do i endure for honor
or fear of fate?

knowing in the end
no matter which path i take
the crown they'll bestow
is a hollow kingdom i rule
alone

Bones

my bones buried beneath brick and mortar
where the roots of my ancestors
overflow

on every sidewalk
each tree whispers my childhood name
and every road winds towards
my final resting place

i can't possess
what was never mine to haunt

but the meek will pray my body
reaches holy land
and the birds will sing my burdens
because they too, understand
what fate begets a forgotten man

Grief

tinnitus in my ear
another train en pass
i stand at the edge of the world
with the sea raging back
spitting truths
that refuse concession
as if the ground could somehow
make me less restless

        hourglass in flux
        i buffer between
        bluffs
        in this deep quiet
        i grieve the ghost of us

Like Her

there were flowers on my window sill
i tried to learn their names
i kept messing it up

i think one
was a sunflower
she didn't say much
but she made her presence known

like her
i wanted to be known too.

The Gap

i leave my front door open
in case your heart remembers the address
and you somehow found your way here

there's a ring in the back of my closet
collecting dust
i vowed on wearing it
but fairytales are meant for movie screens
and these eyes are sunken
staying up all night
watching cloudy skies for shooting stars

i don't believe in destiny anymore
this red string tied to my finger
i tug and pull
yet the gap refuses to close

Red

my anger has no home
it writhes inside my flesh
begs to be given a name
a name other than grief or despair
but all i can think to call it is
red

this red is mine but
neither of us want it

One Second

i always stay past my expiration date
i could never be a firefighter
my commitment to martyrdom
leaves me standing in the doorway
of burning homes

                        one second

                                too long

                                          too late

Regrets

i watch you sitting with your eyes closed
i notice how the nights haunt your days
sometimes you're moving
yet standing in place

in the end
i'll have no regrets
i've tasted death's lips once
i've lived to tell the tale twice

my advice to you:
run
faster than your doubts
further than this dying star

G. LAFAYETTE

II

when you said "i love you too much"
    it left me wondering
how bad is it to love someone like me?

Voices

i can tell by your smile
you hear voices
do they linger in the door
declaring their devotion or
do they keep you awake at night
professing something more?

if only i had been blessed
i wouldn't search for God
in empty rooms

instead i'm forced
to write about love
and how it ends

or about you
and the truth you couldn't
reciprocate
what was never yours

from knife to navel
imbalanced scales course-correct
for all my mistakes that became regrets
for all the crimes i could control
i alone must face this cold

HAD I BECOME THE SUN

if my sacrifice brings justice
maybe in another universe i
won't have to carve your name
on the roof of my mouth
for forgiveness

maybe in another universe
you'd see me as a sinner
worth saving

but when the levees broke
i was already drowning

how much further
would i have had to sink
to earn your praises?

when i fell from grace
i didn't hear voices
no choir or favor
just a fallen angel
blinded by the light
of a smile

i know
you will never be mine to hold

Betrayal

saving you from the ides of march would mean
cutting my face from the frame
on our nightstand

when you came home
i didn't ask where you'd been
but you smelled like a fragrance
i've never had
and in that moment
i knew the end

between childhood innocence
and the failing point
my eyes forgot how to release tears
as if the valve connecting my heart
rusted until it snapped

neighbors called the fire department
demanded somebody put out this flame
that spread coast to coast
i still took the blame

HAD I BECOME THE SUN

solstice turned to equinox and i turned
your deafening silence over
hoping an answer could do more
than haunt me

i grieve a breathing ghost
a thief who keeps my punctured heart
folded in their back pocket for luck

i shame the broken mirror's image
i have betrayed and destroyed myself for

nothing

Holding On

i lay in bed and miss you
it is the under current
throughout my days

covered by the warmth
of memories
heightened by the nights
lingering with regret

i walk this earth
with an open wound and
though i see the end
the goal posts keep moving

tell me
is this hope worth holding on for?

Gone

i miss you in silent moments
when no one is watching
and memories play
of what will never be again

this is all i have left of us
everyone else has moved on

some days i wake up
without reaching across the bed

i know now
you are
gone

Withdrawal

i pour until nothing remains
the memories stain
even after each scar fades

a drop in your sahara
i am a face you struggle to name

you are nicotine in my veins

the withdrawal will kill me
if you don't first

After

my world has fallen apart
and i am here

you left with the stars
and i am here

mourning still came
and i am here

after everything
it is over
and i am here

life is quiet with you gone
and i am here

You (Part I)

i've seen the way your body glows
in the dark
even your scars shine

i'm trying to understand why
you can't stand your own fault lines
but the world won't wait
while you ponder

you count backwards just to fall asleep
you tell me it helps
but it can't stop the deluge
of thoughts you don't say
and i can't help but wonder
what else is at stake

for every person you let in
a thousand truths stay locked out
there's an anchor in your smile
as if you stopped waiting
for search parties
to salvage you
from yourself

HAD I BECOME THE SUN

you say so much
but never what you believe
a puzzle men will turn over
then abandon in defeat

cemeteries don't preserve themselves
and though you're gated
i can peek through the bars
long enough to see fresh flowers
just for you

now birthdays feel different
i reminisce in the kitchen
echoes of stubborn you
restless me

i laugh
and for a moment
you don't feel so far away

i've seen the way your body glows
after everything
your absence softened my soul

Secrets

stained glass window in the corner of the cathedral
they can not help but covet your
abandoned beauty
the way your cracks appear intentional

from an angle you shine
despite the many moons evading you
and your concealed tune

if you were a tapestry or sculpture
maybe then they could figure you out
but you are abstract art
erected in abject terror and awe

stained glass window
solemn secrets only you know

though your story bares it all
only the wide-eyed are willing
to translate your soul

but latin is dead
and my heart

you have been bleeding out for days
in the corner of a cathedral
covered with shallow prayer

Exposed

i thought of people as trees
brash with crown shyness
coyly waiting to be seen
guarded in fear of being exposed

but i wanted to be touched
and i wanted my leaves to be known

my bark smoothed over
as i surrendered to the idea
of being one with the forest

The Message

ground zero wasn't a place
it was a person
distorted in time

i dreamed of a day
where we could be free
but there's a reason the caged birds
sing as these streets grow somber

i am longing for a home
where they have spent centuries
making one out of me

i've been rebooted
and repaired
but never replaced
caution tape and hazard signs
hang across my clavicle
but the message remains the same:

it's easier to keep the truth from someone when
it's hidden in plain sight

Hesitation

please don't hold the doors
there's passengers waiting to get through
i've kept this train running past hours
hoping you'd reach your destination
hoping you'd find joy in the journey
but with each stare
and every second you linger
my heart falters at the stop

i don't know what it is about
you that makes me so nervous
it could be anyone else
a crowded room
a filled out stadium
i could say the words so easily
yet here you are on my train
one foot out with
hesitation
in case a better train
comes and
you no longer care
to see where this line goes

Hope

i play around with the thought in my head
"hope"
as everything around me falls apart
as night turns to day
and i haven't slept in weeks

"hope" that one day the jagged shards
piece me together instead

"hope" when the sun rises so will i

"hope" that forgiveness is a butterfly
landing on my shoulder with gentle conviction

III

faded tattoo on my wrist
a life i thought i would miss
the only thing i want back is myself

G. LAFAYETTE

To Liv

what happens when your delirium is vindicated
when staying awake was the best decision
and
you weren't so crazy after all?

i've been left in burning homes before
convinced i could save us
from the fires you kept setting
but delusion is denial
trying to outrun its own shadow

these issues have become
too serious to sleep off until morning
and
i refuse to die for someone
who refuses to live for me

The Wish | Fate

there's this weight in my chest
i've been straddling a fence
separate timelines
the reality i desire
the one i can never return to

i keep skipping steps
not looking back
in fear i'll find pillars of salt
instead

we only get one wish
so i shouldn't use mine
on someone
or anyone else
knowing what it costs
knowing the price i'll pay

yet i cling to my ideals because
i was this disintegrating star
destined to collide with earth

if my fate is to crash
if either way i must burn
i rather my impact
plant seeds
than turn everything i touch
to ash

You (Part II)

you wanted control so you stayed silent
on that day it snowed
when i froze to death, the coroner said
it was just another broken heart

where do our dreams go when we wake?
i fell asleep mid-day
hoping to find you once i returned
yet lullabies and orchestras only play
towards an end
and in the end i lost myself

our destiny shaped by unrequited needs
born to act out roles in an unending scene
and i never wanted you to suffer
so i never told you to stop

even if you look back
i'd be too late
if you turned around now
i'd be too far gone
there's nothing left for you to mourn

Too Much | Roses

i let the roses cut my hands
it wasn't their fault
it was the thorns

i've always had a nasty habit
of justifying pain
so long as it looks pretty

but there's no honor in suffering
no golden chariots or glory

it's waking up to a bed half empty
seeing your face before the train
gives way

and on the other side stands
absence

i needed a distraction
to numb the ache of knowing

HAD I BECOME THE SUN

nothing in life happens exactly twice

why search for you
under classified listings
missing persons turn to
halfway burnt candles
soundless retching

i am so terribly filled with love
overflowing from the brim
staining every fabric
reminder that

it's possible to have loved
too much

One Day

woke up that morning like nothing was wrong
no one home
the lights were off
but all i heard was this sad song
i didn't question where you'd gone

it could happen any day
any time or any place
in your bed or on a plane
so prepared or blown away
it still happens either way

one day will be yours
the moment this all ends
one day will be yours
where no one plays pretend

one day will be yours
will they come through then?
if one thing is for sure
one day will be yours

HAD I BECOME THE SUN

i felt it nagging on the ride

couldn't see it from outside

there must have been

so many signs

the murder cawing

the bells that chime

or maybe it was words unsaid

the waves that strengthen way too big

the resolve that hardens

the cut i rinse

would you believe it won't make sense?

How To Let Go

i don't know how to let go
the best i can do is
let it be

done holding standards for
people who won't even live up to their own

in a sea full of people
who else sees you like i do?
i won't be there when you find out

The Wall

i keep trying to look
beyond the wall
but i've been the architect
this was supposed to be
my blueprint
my design
and i
keep trying to sacrifice myself for it
when it always planned to save me

i search for someone more qualified
to hold this hollow in my chest
but i've been the composer
the orchestra follows my lead
it's time i conduct

i'm so paranoid
one day you'll find me
and you'll love me
despite my flaws
because it's me who needs to be seen
the reason i could never see
beyond the wall

The Museum

my body is a museum

of all the people i have ever loved

when historians find my remains

i want to be remembered

for all the wonders i held

not the tragedies left behind

Lilith

had i become the sun

every surface i touched would have burned

but letting you go will be my last act of love

history will immortalize my light as

Lilith

Epilogue

if i must suffer
i'll make meaning of this
too

The Sun

the sun woke me up
again
some people won't see today
someday i won't see a tomorrow
but

the sun woke me up again
it thawed my heart and i moved on
just like you said
then

the sun woke me up again
and for once
everything i touched felt
vibrant

the sun woke me up again

and i finally understood
all the lengths love will go

until we meet again

Acknowledgements

My One, for being the lightest air, the ever-burning flame that kept me warm during my coldest nights, and the embodiment of unconditional love. You are the rhythm beneath every word.

Norah, for being the lantern gently guiding my path when the way grew dim, for proving that some friendships are so strong they transcend lifetimes. You gave more than just wisdom, you gave hope.

Ace, for always being down to dig deeper, for supporting me with every pivot.

Heather, for picking up the phone every-time, for never flinching at my bleeding heart.

Isa, for sitting with my late-night spirals, for making the silence feel safe.

Allie, for fervently believing in my ramblings, for holding every word with care.

Assata, for reading my rawest thoughts without judgement, for reminding me grace still exists.

Chai, for catching my thoughts as they spilled, for understanding all the things I didn't say.

Jazz, for reading every last minute revision with compassion, for never making me feel like I was too much.

Monica, for reading between the lines, for offering perspective I didn't know I needed.

To you, the readers, for walking with me through this fleeting moment. for the honor of us crossing paths.

Thank you.

G.

G. LAFAYETTE

About the Author

G. Lafayette was born in New Rochelle, New York, and has been drawn to the written word for as long as they can remember. In 2011, they began writing poetry and prose as a way to give shape to emotions too complex to speak aloud.

Through free verse, Lafayette explores the stream of consciousness, layering parables, metaphors, analogies, and allegory to create meaning from memory, emotion, and imagination. They can often be found with a cup of tea in hand, disappearing into the presence of loved ones or wandering the hidden spaces between silence and wonder—always listening, always writing.

www.ingramcontent.com/pod-product-compliance
Lightning Source LLC
Chambersburg PA
CBHW070858050426
42453CB00012B/2260